1734

D1632038

Hello to Riding

Hello to Riding

Jane Allen and Mary Danby

Illustrated by Alison Prince

Heinemann : London

William Heinemann Ltd
10 Upper Grosvenor Street, London W1X 9PA
LONDON MELBOURNE TORONTO
JOHANNESBURG AUCKLAND

First published 1980
Text © Jane Allen and Mary Danby 1980
Illustrations © Alison Prince 1980

434 92701 5

Set, printed and bound in Great Britain by
Fakenham Press Limited, Fakenham, Norfolk

Contents

Wanting to Ride

When did you first know that you wanted to ride?

Perhaps you became fascinated by ponies after seeing them in fields near your home, or reading books about them. Maybe you were brought up with horses, and sat on a pony before you could walk. Or you might have been taken to a riding school by your parents – or simply found that you enjoyed the feeling of riding a pony or donkey at the seaside.

People have all sorts of different reasons for wanting to ride. Some like the wonderful exercise it gives you, and the fresh air, the chance to see new places, the excitement of being carried by an animal. Some learn to ride so that they can win competitions. This is fine, so long as they remember that it's always more important to ride well than to win.

It's fun to be able to go out with friends on their ponies, and enjoy doing things together, like exploring the countryside.

Some people want to be able to show off, and this is understandable, because sitting on top of a horse or pony does make you feel rather proud – especially if you are both looking smart and moving nicely. But it's a pride you should share with your pony, and be grateful for your luck in having the chance to ride.

Children sometimes like to use their ponies to play games on, such as Cowboys and Indians. Make sure that the ponies enjoy it, too, then you can all have fun.

Of course, some people are just "pony mad". They simply want to be with ponies – watching them, handling them, loving and caring for them, riding them and forgetting everything else for a while in their enjoyment and companionship.

But nearly everyone who wants to ride does so for a little bit of all these reasons.

To become a good rider, you must want to "get together" with your pony, learning to understand him and help him, so that you will both enjoy the lessons and games.

Learn to notice what kind of pony you are riding – bold, nervous, willing, mischievous, kind, stubborn, gentle ... and how he is feeling – lively or tired, contented or uncomfortable, friendly, bored or irritable. You can begin to sense these feelings the first time you go for a ride, even just a short walk around a paddock. Everything you discover about ponies is part of the understanding that you can go on adding to all your life.

If you are lucky enough to have a pony bought for you, or are allowed to choose from several at a riding school, you will probably want the pony that you feel best on – usually because he makes you feel safe and confident and seems happy to do what you want him to. His willingness to do what he is told is partly because he is a nice "person", but mainly because he has been properly trained. If he is difficult, pushing or pulling you around, or treading on your toes, or walking away when you want to get on, he has either been badly trained or has not yet been trained enough.

A pony should have learnt to be well-behaved by the time he is five years old. However, at that age he is still young and inexperienced enough to be surprised or upset when he meets something new, like a rattling lorry, or a loudspeaker, or a pack of hounds. He still needs a lot of help to get used to new things, so an experienced person should always be with you to calm him down.

An older pony will probably have changed owners several times and will have been to all kinds of places and done many different things. He is likely to be safer for a beginner to handle – for one thing, he probably won't be bothered by traffic. However, some older ponies will have been ridden carelessly at some time, and may have learnt a few bad habits, like laziness or pulling.

This pony is too small for this rider.

Try to find a pony that is the right size for you. He must be able to carry your weight easily. Very small ponies can be difficult to ride, because your balance has to be very good to cope with their quick little movements, and big ones may be too strong and hard to handle.

This pony is too big.

So you can see that, when choosing a pony – to buy, or just to ride for an hour – there's more to it than just picking the prettiest or the most appealing. The pony for you is the one that *feels* right – safe and easy to manage. Learn to ride him well, and *you* will feel right for *him*.

This pony is just right.

What You Should Wear for Riding

For handling ponies, and riding them, some clothes are much safer, tidier and more comfortable than others.

If you want to look particularly smart – if you are riding in a show, for instance – you will need special clothes. When you are simply riding at home, you can, if you like, wear something more casual.

Casual clothes   Special clothes

Whatever else you may be wearing, a *hard hat* is a must. But it has to fit well – a hat which wobbles about is of no use at all. A chin strap which goes over the hat and holds it in place is very helpful. If properly fitted, it should stop you chattering or chewing!

Riding trousers are called *jodhpurs*. They are specially made to allow you to stretch your legs apart and to stop them being pinched or rubbed. If you have no jodhpurs, make sure your trousers are thick enough to protect your legs. Sometimes, you will see people wearing *riding breeches*. These are like short-legged jodhpurs and are worn with boots.

Riding boots, made of leather or rubber, are excellent, of course, and so are the shorter *jodhpur boots*, but ordinary walking shoes with good heels and smooth sides are also fine. Leather boots or shoes help protect your feet if you get trodden on.

These are bad:

- shoes with wedge heels, or no heels at all. Your feet can slip forwards through the stirrups.
- shoes with buckles. They can catch on the stirrups.
- shoes or boots with big ridges on the bottom. You cannot slide your feet in or out of the stirrups easily.
- shoes that are floppy, like plimsolls or open-topped sandals, which do not give you any support or protection.

Riding boots

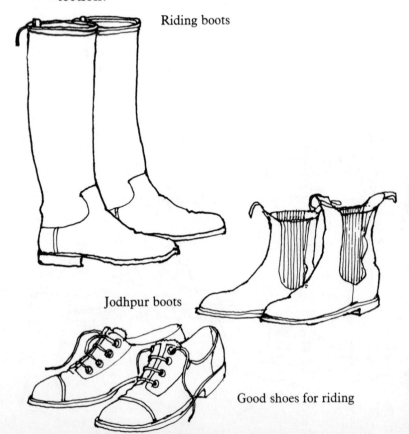

Jodhpur boots

Good shoes for riding

If you have nothing else that is suitable, Wellington boots can be all right, but they must fit properly and have smooth soles and good heels.

Don't ride in muddy boots. Not only will you look scruffy, but the mud might scratch the saddle.

Remember gloves in the winter. Frozen fingers can't work very well and may stop you concentrating on your riding. Proper "string" gloves – especially those with woollen backs – are ideal, and thinner gloves can be very smart when worn in the summer for shows.

You should always try to be neat and tidy – not just for smartness, but because it's safer.

Ties should be pinned down. Hair should be neatly tied back. Belts, zips and buttons should be done up. Zips on anoraks can be an awful nuisance as they can sometimes scratch your saddle, especially when you are dismounting. Never wear anything that hangs down or trails behind you – like a scarf. And beware of dangling hoods – they can catch on branches.

So – don't be a slapdash rider in slapdash, dangerous clothes.

Wearing the right clothes, and being neat and tidy, will help you to ride better. You will sit up tall and proud, feeling smart and looking fit to be in charge of your pony.

Saddles and Bridles

When you're learning to ride properly, which means safely, in a good, comfortable position, your pony must have all the right equipment. Saddles and bridles – and anything else we put on a pony for riding – are called *tack*. Tack is made mainly of leather, and the person who makes and mends it is called a *saddler*.

The *bridle* helps you to control and guide your pony.

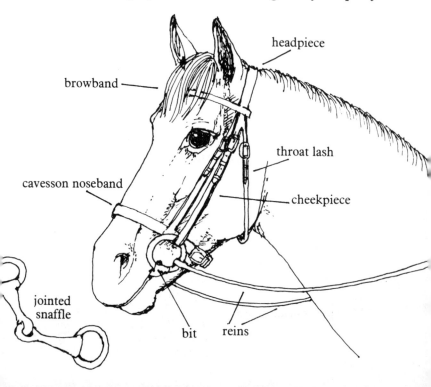

headpiece

browband

throat lash

cavesson noseband

cheekpiece

jointed snaffle

bit   reins

The *bit* is a metal or rubber bar, often with a joint in the middle, which goes into the pony's mouth. By using the *reins*, which are attached to the rings of the bit, you can send all kinds of messages to the pony, who can feel even the smallest movement of the bit and bridle. There are many different kinds of bit, but the one you will probably see most often is a jointed *snaffle*.

The *headpiece* and *cheekpieces* keep the bit at the right height in the pony's mouth.

The *browband* and *throat lash* stop the bridle slipping backwards or forwards. The *noseband* can be an ordinary one – a cavesson – or a "dropped" one, carefully fitted below the bit.

It is important that your pony should wear the right kind of *saddle* – one that is comfortable for him as well as for you.

Some small children with small ponies have saddles made of thick felt. Some have saddles which are really just a big leather pad. Both of these are bendy and will fit almost any shape of pony, but because they have no "tree" – the frame inside a saddle – they are not very helpful to the rider.

To ride in the correct, balanced position, you need the help of a good saddle – one with a tree that is the right size and shape for your pony. This spreads the rider's weight evenly over the pony's back and protects his backbone.

The *girth* is the pony's "belt", holding the saddle in place.

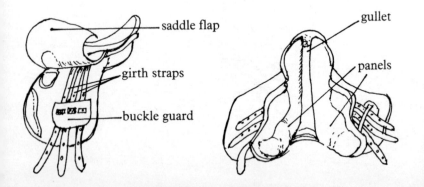

saddle flap

girth straps

buckle guard

gullet

panels

Ordinary stirrup   Safety stirrup

Stirrups should be big enough to allow the rider's foot to move easily in and out, but not so big that the whole foot can slip through.

Stirrup leathers should always be buckled on the outside, away from the saddle, and the buckles slid up to the top, so that they are covered by the skirt and can't hurt your legs.

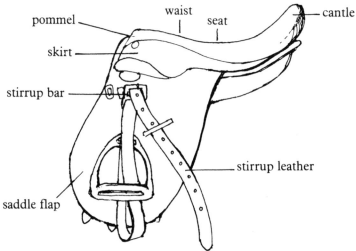

Choosing the right tack for your pony, and fitting it properly, is something you *must* have expert help with. Unsuitable or badly fitting tack can cause pain by rubbing or pinching. An uncomfortable, unhappy pony would not be safe to ride.

Cleaning Your Tack

Good tack is expensive, so you must look after it carefully, never leaving it lying on the ground or out in the rain.

New leather is rather stiff, and it has to be softened with saddle soap and special oil, so that the straps and buckles become easy to do up and undo. Old leather, which has not been cared for, gets so dried out that it will crack and break.

When tack is worn by a pony, it gets dirty with sweat, grease and dust out of his coat – often mud splashes, too. Apart from looking scruffy, if dirty tack is not cleaned regularly, it will cause sore places.

Wear old clothes or an apron and begin by undoing all the buckles and other fastenings – you may need help. While you are doing this, check that none of the stitching has come undone.

Take a damp sponge and wipe over all the leather to remove the dirt, which can damage it and stop the saddle soap getting into it.

Remember that leather is easily damaged by water or heat, so don't use hot water on it, or soak it, or put it somewhere hot to dry.

Use a clean, damp sponge with the saddle soap to wipe it on to the leather and rub it in. Besides cleaning and softening, the saddle soap helps to keep the rain and dirt out and leaves a nice shine.

If your girth is not made of leather, it may need brushing or scrubbing.

Clean the bit and stirrups by scrubbing them, then use metal polish (but not on the mouthpiece of the bit).

Ask someone to show you how to put everything back together, then hang your bridle tidily on a peg and put your saddle away on a rail or saddle "horse".

Carry a bridle like this . . .

Tacking Up

How to put on your saddle and bridle

Saddles can be heavy and difficult to carry, so you'll probably want to fetch the saddle and bridle separately.

Carry the bridle to the pony and hang it up or lay it down somewhere clean and safe – perhaps on a nearby bale. Make sure that your pony cannot reach it to chew it, or knock it down, or tread on it. Ponies will usually fiddle with anything they can touch.

. . . not like this!

Now fetch the saddle and put it down carefully near the pony, in a safe place, where it cannot fall and break its tree, or be scratched.

Carry a saddle like this . . .

. . . not like this!

Tacking up is not very easy for beginners, so you should have someone to help you. It's a good idea to watch how it's done before having a go yourself. A saddle or bridle which has been put on badly can be very uncomfortable for the pony, and unsafe, too. Take your time, think about what you're doing, and talk gently to your pony while you are handling him. Always move around his head, rather than his hind legs, so that you are safe and in control of him at all times.

Putting On the Saddle

Your pony should be tied up, with your helper standing by his head. Some ponies can be ticklish when they first feel the saddle, and might even want to turn around and nip you. They must be handled gently but firmly.

Let your pony sniff the saddle, if he wants to, before you put it on. Don't suddenly bang it on his back – he would get quite a shock.

Stand by his nearside (left) shoulder and lift the saddle on to the end of his mane. You may need help to do this. Now slide it back into the right place, just behind – but well clear of – his withers. If you have a numnah, make sure it is not creased or pressing on the backbone.

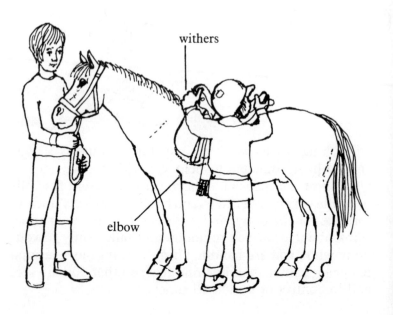

withers

elbow

Your helper can put a hand on the saddle to keep it still while you go round to the offside.

Lift the girth down carefully, so that it doesn't bang your pony's legs, and leave it hanging close to his elbow. Now lift the saddle flap and check that nothing is twisted or turned under. Make sure the buckle guard is pulled down over the buckles, as it's there to stop the inside of the flap being scratched or dented.

Back on the near side, stretch an arm underneath your pony to take hold of the girth. Most ponies don't mind this at all, but if you are nervous, ask for help.

Bring the girth towards you, making sure it isn't twisted, lift the saddle flap and do up the buckles, front strap first.

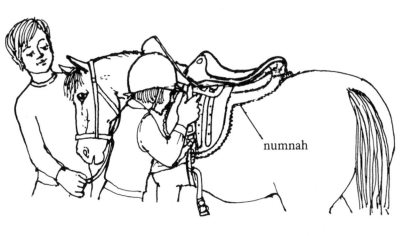

numnah

Don't tighten the girth too much to begin with. Slide your fingers under the girth, from the front, to check it's just tight enough to keep the saddle from slipping, and to make sure there are no creases in the pony's skin.

Putting On the Bridle

Place the reins over your pony's head. Take off his head-collar and buckle it loosely around his neck, so that he can't move away. Hold his head still with your right hand, then lift the bridle and take hold of it by the cheek straps. Feel your pony's lips with your hand and gently slide the bit in. If he doesn't open his mouth for you, ask someone to help you.

Keep gently lifting the bridle until the bit is in the right place, resting against the corners of his mouth.

Now change hands, so that you can put the headpiece over his ears. Bring his ears carefully through the space above the browband, and pull his forelock through, too.

Check that the bridle is comfortably in place – not lopsided or pressing on the base of his ears – and with the bit just wrinkling the corners of his lips. Alter the buckles if you need to.

Do up the throat lash and cavesson noseband loosely enough to give the pony freedom to move. If you can easily swing two fingers under them, that is about right.

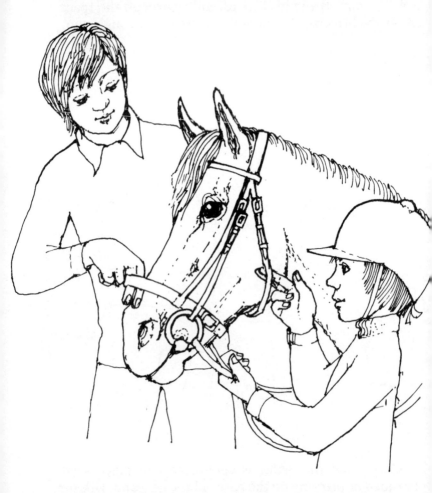

Lastly, make sure the ends of all the straps are tucked tidily into their "keepers", not left to flap about.

If this is the first time you have put on tack, it will have taken quite a while, but it is better to be slow and careful. Don't practise on a pony who doesn't like having his tack put on – you need a quiet, calm pony to help you to learn to get it right.

If you want to leave your pony tacked up while you go and get ready for your ride, put his reins over the saddle and under the stirrup leathers, so that they can't dangle near his feet. Undo the throat lash and do it up again around the reins, then replace the headcollar over the bridle.

Mounting and Dismounting
(which means getting on – and getting off)

First of all, go to your pony's head, speaking quietly to him and letting him sniff you. Perhaps someone else put on his tack, or you have changed your jacket since he last saw you. Give him a chance to recognise you.

To lead him out of the stable, unbuckle the headcollar and release the reins from the throat lash, then take the reins from under the stirrups and pass them over his head. Stand on his near side and, with your right hand, take hold of both reins underneath his chin. The rest of the reins should be held in a big loop in your left hand.

Say "Walk on" in a firm voice and push your pony's head away from you to lead him out. Don't tug him towards you. If he is in a stall, move slowly to give him time to turn around carefully. You don't want him to squash you against the wall.

Always go through the middle of doorways or gateways, because a pony usually allows room for his own body, but not for tack. A rider's knees can be scraped, too. So, as you approach a narrow space, think ahead – and aim for the middle.

When your pony first comes out of his stable, he feels rather like you do when you get out of bed in the morning – probably a bit stiff and dopey. So walk him round for a minute or two to help him relax and loosen up a little. Don't let him put his head down to graze. This is a bad habit which he should not learn.

If you are a very new beginner, your teacher or helper will have got the pony ready for you with the reins lying on his neck. Before mounting, untuck the stirrup leathers to slide the stirrups down – don't just drag them.

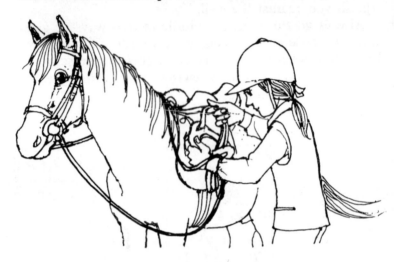

To find out if the stirrups are about the correct length for you when you're riding, put the knuckle of your right hand against the buckle. The stirrup should reach your right armpit. (Do this with your left arm through the reins, so that you are always in control of your pony and have both hands free for altering the buckle if necessary.)

Make sure the offside stirrup is the same length as the nearside one.

One last thing before you mount – *tighten your girth*. You will need help to pull up the girth straps, but when it is done, check again, so that you can learn the difference. Ponies and horses should be girthed up gently, so that they are not made uncomfortable.

To mount by yourself, stand on your pony's near side, and, with your right hand, pick up your reins by the buckle. Now slide your left hand up the reins. This way, they will both be the same length and you will be able to control your pony while you mount. If you are carrying a small whip, this should be in your left hand, together with the reins.

As well as the reins, take up a handful of your pony's mane, so that you don't pull on his mouth. Stand with your back to his head and put your left foot well into the stirrup.

Move your right hand up to the waist or pommel of the saddle – not the cantle, because you'll twist the saddle out of position. Keep your bent knee firm – don't let it wobble.

With a little hop on your right foot, turn to face the saddle, then step strongly up on to your left foot, swinging your right leg over the saddle.

Try not to touch your pony's back with your foot, as ponies can be frightened by that.

Settle into place – try not to crash down on to the saddle.

If you have to use a *mounting block* (a platform you can stand on to help you reach the stirrup), make sure it's strong and solid.

Another way to mount, if you are rather small for your pony, is to be given a *leg-up*. (This is how jockeys get on to racehorses.)

Take up the reins as before, together with a handful of mane. Face the saddle and put your right hand on the waist of the saddle – or as high up as you can reach. Lift up your left foot behind you, but keep the rest of your body firm and straight. Your helper will now lift your

... and the wrong way!

bent leg and push you up straight, while you give a little hop. Remember to keep your head up and not collapse in the middle. Swing your right leg over the saddle, and you're there.

Try not to let your pony move at all while you are mounting. He should stay absolutely still until you are ready to go.

To *dismount*, put both your reins in your left hand and rest it on your pony's neck. Take both feet out of the stirrups. Lean forward slightly and place your right hand on the pommel, then swing your leg over the back of the saddle.

Bring your legs neatly together, then land gently on the near side, bending your knees.

Never dismount by stepping off, with one foot in the stirrup, or by swinging your leg over the pony's mane. You may see other people do it, but it's very dangerous.

Once you are on top, move your right foot around to feel for the stirrup. Try not to look down, as this makes you wobbly.

With your reins still in one hand, pat your pony – let him know you've mounted safely and are ready to enjoy riding him. Stroke his shiny summer coat, or bury your fingers in his thick winter hair. See how his ears look from behind. Are they flicking to and fro, waiting for your signals?

When you're ready to ride off, take one rein in each hand. With your thumbs nearest your body, put your hands down on to the reins – your teacher will show you how – and then bring your elbows into your sides. Turn your thumbs to the top.

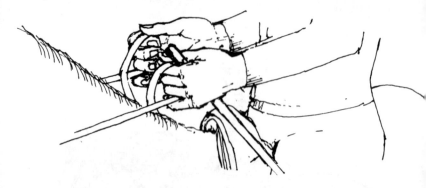

Hold the reins lightly and let them slide through your hands a little until they are the same length. Make sure they aren't twisted.

Wriggle your seat deep into the middle of the saddle, sit up tall and straight – and be proud to be there.

First Lessons

A Good Beginning

It is worth taking the trouble to learn to ride properly, right from the start. Not only will you and your pony be safer and more comfortable with each other, but you will have a lot more fun.

To be a good rider, you must *move with your pony*. You've probably seen, from time to time, a pony setting off before his rider is ready. The rider loses his balance and is "left behind" – sometimes falling off, even.

44

So, the first lesson is *Think before you move*. Think about going forward, about preparing your pony for what you want him to do, then you will move off smoothly together.

The Right Position

Once you are in the saddle, you and your pony are a team. A good rider sits so easily on his pony that he seems almost a part of it. Some people are naturally better balanced than others, but by learning a good riding position at the beginning, your balance is helped enormously. No part of you should be stiff – you should try always to be relaxed, which means your muscles should be soft and easy, not tight and strained.

Sit up straight and square (not lopsided), facing forwards. Keep your head up all the time – don't look down. Your legs should be right underneath the rest of your body (not stuck forwards or pulled back), with your hip, knee and ankle joints bent. Your lower leg should hang straight down, and your toes should face the front, with your heels down and the ball of your foot resting on the stirrup – don't push your whole foot "home". Your arms should be hanging by your sides, with the elbows bent and the wrists straight.

There are all sorts of exercises you can do to loosen up your muscles and improve your position. You can learn about them later in the book. They are all about moving different parts of your body and then returning to this tall, level and relaxed position.

Using the Aids

But a good rider doesn't just sit there, like a lazy passenger – he learns to control the pony's movements. The ways in which you "talk" to your pony, telling him what you want, are called *aids*.

One of the most important aids is your *voice*. When a pony is very young, a lot of his teaching is done by voice, so he will understand a calm, slow voice to settle him down, or a quick, lively voice to wake him up a bit. A long "Whoa" (which is "wo-o-o" when you say it) will usually slow him down or stop him. Don't expect him to stop dead – try to make any change in movement smooth and steady. A quick, firm "Walk on!" or "Trot!" (say "ter-rot" to make it very clear) will tell him to get a move on.

As well as your voice, your *legs* and your *body* help you to urge on your pony or slow him down. Send him forward by sitting well down and tapping his sides with the flat insides of your legs.

Don't give big, flappy kicks, where your legs come off the saddle.

To control and guide your pony, you also need to use your *hands*. Even the smallest movements of your hands will send messages along the reins. It's a way of saying to your pony "Slow down", "Begin to turn", "Have a stretch ..." and so on. Try to learn how gentle or firm your messages need to be.

To *shorten* your reins, put both reins in one hand and slide your free hand further up the rein. This hand now takes both reins, while the other rein is shortened. Separate your hands and make sure your pony's neck is straight and the reins are even. Don't take your hands off the reins, and don't try to shorten them by wriggling your fingers along them.

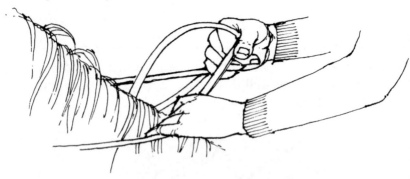

To *lengthen* them, just open your fingers and let the reins slide through.

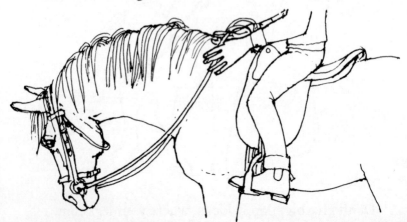

To *slow down or stop*, "feel" your pony's mouth by an extra bending of your fingers and arms. But your hands are only a part of the "stop" message. While the reins hold the bit steady and level in your pony's mouth, push down with your seat and give a squeeze with your legs. Say a long, low "Whoa-oa", and he should obey you willingly. This is how you slow down from any pace.

Your hands and your legs are partners. Always use them together.

Your *whip* is another of the aids. If your pony won't go forward after you have asked him firmly and repeatedly with your voice and legs, put both reins in one hand and hit him once, hard, behind your leg, to send him on. Look ahead of you, not back at the whip.

At the beginning, use your whip only when your teacher tells you, otherwise you might get into the habit of using it instead of your legs.

Your voice and your whip are also used to punish your pony when he has done something wrong. A harsh "No!" or a growl, and a quick slap of the whip – if he had tried to bite another pony, for instance – would be part of his teaching. But it's also important to remember to pat his neck and say "Good pony!" if he has done well. That is how he learns what is good and what is bad, and what is expected of him.

Riding Forwards

Your teacher will have helped you to adjust the stirrup leathers to the right length.

The bottom of the stirrup should come just below your ankle bone when your leg is hanging down.

You will also be shown how to hold the reins (not so long and floppy that you can't feel the pony's mouth, nor so short and tight that the pony wants to pull free from you). They should make a straight line from the bit to your hands, held just above and just in front of the saddle.

52

Reins and stirrups too short . . .

. . . too long . . .

. . . just right.

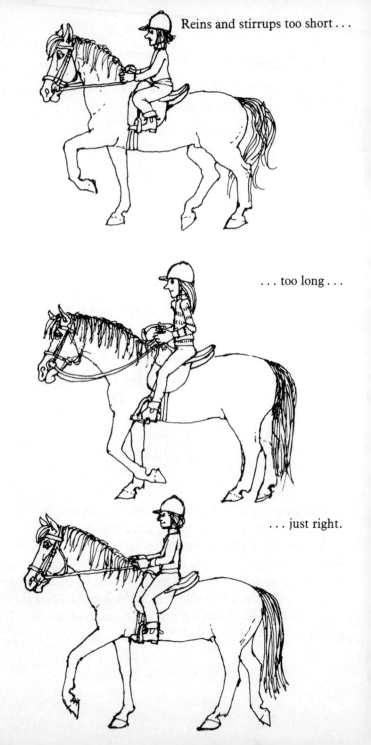

A *neck strap* is a big help if you are a beginner and feel you need something firm to hold on to.

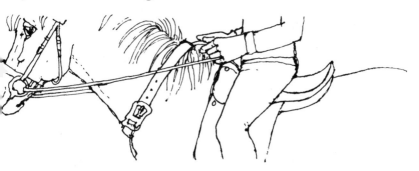

For first lessons, you will have a *leading rein* attached to the pony's cavesson noseband. Until you have learnt how to give your pony the right messages, by using the aids properly, you will need a lot of help from your teacher. However, when you are ready to go forward, it is you who will give a squeeze with both legs to warn him: "We are going to do something." Now say firmly "Walk on!" and give a few little kicks to urge him forwards.

Move your hands slightly away from you to allow your pony to step forward. It's called "giving with your hands". This also helps you to move your body forwards a little, to go with him.

As your pony walks calmly on, enjoy the rocking feeling. Let your arms follow the nodding movement of his head and neck. Soon, you'll find you can count "One, two, three, four" in time with his steps. The smallest ponies usually have the quickest steps.

Your first walks will help you get used to the "feel" of your pony. Every pony is different – every saddle, too. Use your legs to keep him striding out. Don't let him dawdle.

When you are ready to halt, ask him to stop correctly, with "a leg at each corner" by using your hands, legs and seat to shorten his body, as if you were pushing him up against an invisible wall.

Practise starting and halting several times, saying a firm "Walk on!" and a long "Whoa-oa". If your pony is helpful and obedient, reward him with patting.

When you have to turn a corner, remember that a pony has a long body – not an upright one like yours – and needs to be helped to do it smoothly. Sit up straight and have an even "feel" on both reins. Lead the pony's head and neck round, with your inside rein held a little away from your pony's neck.

Use both legs to send your pony forward, but push a little harder with the inside leg, to "bend" his body round it. As he goes around the corner, the pony's body should be curved like a banana, not flat and stiff.

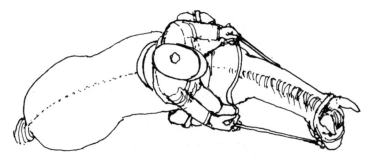

56

Sooner or later, your teacher may put you on a *lungeing rein*. This is much longer than a leading rein, and is attached to the front of the cavesson. On the end of a lungeing rein, you can ride round in large circles while your teacher stands in the middle, holding a long whip to help with the pony's forward movement. Riding on the lunge, you can concentrate on getting your position right and sitting deep in the saddle – sometimes without stirrups – because your teacher has control of the pony.

Trotting

When you have got used to riding at the walk, you will want to try trotting.

Wait for your teacher to say "Prepare to trot", then shorten your reins a little. At the walk, a pony gently nods his head in time with his steps, but at the trot he shortens his neck a bit and keeps his head still.

Give a squeeze with your legs, to tell your pony: "We're about to do something else." Now give little kicks with both legs to send him forwards, and say firmly: "Ter-rot!" If he is a lazy pony, your teacher can help, but try not to jerk into a trot.

The movement of the trot is quite different from the walk. You can feel the legs going one-two, one-two, in a steady rhythm.

You should sit tall, but slightly forward. Holding the neck strap will help you do this during your first lessons. Keep your head high and pretend you are a cowboy jogging slowly into town. Let your legs hang soft and long, and feel your seat going gently bump, bump, bump on the saddle.

Don't trot for too long, or your helper will be exhausted! Slow down by squeezing with your legs and taking a firmer hold on both reins. If you are using the neck strap, you need not drop it. A pull on the neck strap as you push into the saddle will slow down most ponies. Sit tall, with your head up, and remember the "Whoa-oa . . ."

Put both reins in one hand and give your pony a firm pat on the neck with the other . . . "Good pony." Open your fingers to let the pony have a stretch – and have a good wriggle yourself.

As you do more trotting, the changes from walk to trot and trot to walk will become smoother. Relax in the saddle, with your shoulders down – not hunched up or stiff. This is called the *sitting trot*. You can help yourself to sit deep in the saddle by practising slipping your feet in and out of the stirrups, while sitting up straight.

Try keeping time with your pony's steps, by saying out loud: "Bump, bump, bump, bump." When you can feel the rhythm very clearly, say: "One, two, one, two," instead, and then, ready for the next stage, say: "Up, down, up, down."

This is how to learn the *rising trot*. You can practise it first while your pony is standing still. Hold on to the neck strap or mane, and stand up in your stirrups, then try to do this in time to your teacher's voice saying: "Up, down, up, down." Your body should rise forwards on the "Up", as your pony will be going forwards. On "Down", let yourself gently down on to the saddle again.

The rising trot   Up ...

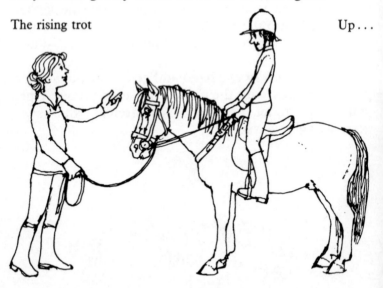

You will start slowly, then your teacher will gradually quicken the words, until you are rising at about the right speed for your pony's trot.

When you can do this comfortably, try it at the walk, still holding the mane or neck strap so that you don't pull at your pony's mouth.

You're ready now to try the rising trot. Always begin with a sitting trot, so that you are close to the pony. Feel the rhythm: bump, bump, bump, bump. Now say: "Up, down, up, down," and see if you can go with the movement of your pony. It's a lovely, swinging feeling when bits of it are right.

Don't tire yourself out. Return to the sitting trot for a while, then try rising again. It doesn't matter if you don't get it right straight away. It's much better to go smoothly forwards with the pony, rising or gently bumping, than to struggle too hard and bang about in the saddle.

. . . Down

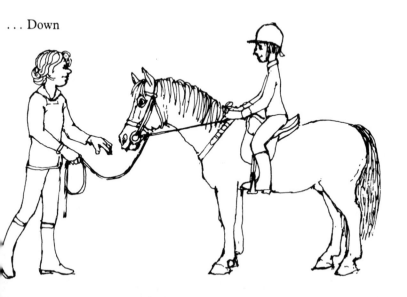

When you can manage a good rising trot off the leading rein, keeping a steady rhythm, you're ready to go on to *trotting poles*. These are thick, straight poles placed on the ground for you to ride over: a very good exercise for your pony – and you.

Begin by walking over one pole. Ride straight at it and step over the middle. Your pony will lower his head to look at it, and may even sniff it. Let your hands go forward with the reins and hold on to the mane or neck strap. Give your pony a squeeze with your legs, to say: "Keep on walking", but no big kicks, or he might think you want him to do a big jump! Your body should go forwards with the pony, and remember to keep your head up, looking in front of you, not down at the pole.

When you've walked over the pole, shorten your reins, turn around and come back over it.

Your helper can now put another two poles on the ground, so that there are three altogether. For a small pony, they should be spaced about the length of three ladies' feet apart. Never put just two poles down, because, to a pony, they would look too much like a jump.

Ride round again and walk over your three poles in exactly the same way: step, step, step. Your pony will look down to inspect this new obstacle, so your hands must follow. Once more – body forward, head high, and look in front of you. Keep your heels well down and your toes facing forwards. This is what will later become your jumping position.

When you and your pony are happy walking over the poles, try trotting over them. It's important to remember that the pony reaches further with his trotting strides, so the poles must be moved another foot (about 30 cms) or so apart. Get your pony trotting steadily first, then ride straight towards the poles at the rising trot. Bounce, bounce, bounce, the pony goes, and you try to keep your forward position and your "up, down" rhythm.

Over the poles, he picks up his feet higher than usual, bending his knee and hock joints more and using the muscles of his back. Push him with your legs to keep him moving forwards with lively steps.

Learning to trot well takes many hours of riding, but by the time you can manage the exercise of trotting poles you will be well on the way to becoming a capable rider.

Hacking

Once you feel quite safe and happy at the walk, and have begun trotting lessons, it's good to spend some of your riding time going out hacking around the countryside.

This is very enjoyable, helping you to relax and look around you while getting on with your riding. For instance, you will soon find that you can shorten your reins while watching cattle in the next field – or you might suddenly realise you're doing a very nice rising trot while admiring the wild flowers along the hedge.

If your pony is feeling a bit too lively, he can first be lunged for a little while, until he has settled down enough for you to get on and start riding.

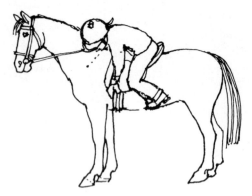

Once you are in the saddle, make sure that you are comfortable. Check that your girth is tight enough by leaning down and wriggling your fingers under it.

Is your jacket done up? Is your hat level, with its chin strap in place? Will you need gloves? It's worth thinking about comfort beforehand – you don't want to spoil a good ride by being too cold or by having to dismount and "spend a penny".

Whether you're hacking with a small group from the riding school, or perhaps with just one experienced person, you will need to begin on a leading rein, to make you feel safe and under control. The rein will usually be held by another rider, because it's very tiring for a leader to be on foot.

Try to stay at the side of the person leading you. Send your pony on – don't let him lag behind, dragging on the leading rein. The rein is there for safety – not for pulling you along.

When you have to cross a road, everyone on the ride should halt together in a group. Remember the rules: stop, look and listen. The leader will decide when it is safe to cross, and you should then all move together, crossing the road as quickly and calmly as possible.

If part of your hack is along a road, keep in to the side, one behind the other and close together. If you carry a whip, it should be on the side away from the hedge, to help keep the pony in.

When traffic comes along, *always* send your pony firmly forwards. Stopping or turning round in the road is dangerous. If a big lorry approaches, the leader may signal it to slow down and wait while you move off the road into a gateway.

Most ponies are used to traffic and will walk calmly on, taking no notice, but you should always keep both hands on the reins and send your pony on in a straight line. If a driver slows down for you, don't try and wave a "thank you" unless you are well in control – just call out your thanks or smile and nod your head.

When you reach a grassy lane or woodland track, don't always trot straight away. Your pony will get into the habit of doing that every time, whether you want to or not.

Woods are interesting places to ride through, so keep your pony steady and don't let him get excited. Watch out for low branches. The peak of your cap will help to protect your face, but you may have to lean down towards the pony's neck, turning your face slightly to one side. Keep your toes turned in, so that they don't get caught up.

Keep an eye open for tree roots and stumps and rabbit holes. It's safest to stick to the main track through the woods. You will notice the different sound your pony's feet make on the soft path, and he may move with a longer stride.

If you've done quite a bit of riding, and feel happy at the trot, this may be a good time to have your first proper canter. Give your pony time to settle down and be moving smoothly, then find a straight part of the track, slightly uphill.

To prepare to canter, shorten your reins and hold a handful of the mane. Push your heels down and give little kicks with both legs, saying firmly: "Can-ter!" As your pony begins to canter, you will feel his stride change from the "one-two, one-two" of trotting, to "one-two-three, one-two-three". Beginners should lean forward a little and stand up in their stirrups – rather like a jockey. Your pony will be moving forwards in little bounds: a lovely, bouncy feeling, so keep your head high and enjoy it.

At the end of the straight bit of path, the leader will warn you to slow to a trot, so sit back and down in the saddle. That should be enough to get your pony to break into a trot again, and you will swing into your rising trot rhythm. If your pony needs a stronger message, squeeze with both legs and pull gently on the reins, saying "Who-ooa". When you have slowed down, give him a good pat for taking care of you.

It's fun to look out for small logs and ditches to step over and across, and for low banks to ride up and down. These little exercises will make the ride more interesting for your pony, too.

To ride *uphill*, lean forward a little, keeping your head up and your hands slightly forwards.

Going *downhill*, sit up very straight and level, with your feet slightly more forwards than usual. If your pony wants to lower his head, lengthen the reins a little by letting them slide through your fingers. Collect up your reins again as the ground flattens out.

Sometimes a pony will want to go faster downhill, but, by squeezing with both legs and steadying with your hands, you can tell him not to hurry.

When you're riding through undergrowth, don't try to make your pony go among prickly plants or nettles, because if he is fine-skinned he will feel their stings as much as you would.

It's important always to try and ride straight through puddles, rather than go round them. If your pony gets into the habit of avoiding them, you may find him stepping out into traffic, or suddenly moving sideways while you're cantering through a wood, bruising your leg against a tree.

Some ponies may shy when you're out hacking. Shying means suddenly moving away from something – a dog, for instance, or a flapping flag – so that you are taken by surprise and may lose your balance. If a pony shies out of fright, try to make him feel confident and safe. Use your

voice calmly to tell him it's all right, and keep your reins short, driving him strongly forwards, past whatever has alarmed him. If he can feel that *you* are not frightened, this will help him a lot.

If your pony shies off the road on to someone's private lawn, do try to say sorry and perhaps tread down any marks he's made. Always respect other people's property while out hacking. Where possible, keep to paths and tracks, and to the sides of farmers' fields – apart from anything else, you don't want to make people dislike ponies. And it's also important to remember good manners to other riders – like not going ahead if another rider has to stop for something, not pushing past through a small gap, or going so fast that the smallest pony can't keep up.

Don't hold back...

If your pony is lively, don't try to hold him back – this almost *makes* him buck or "fly jump". You will have the smoothest ride if you let him keep up. (However, don't charge up to the back of other ponies and upset them.)

When your pony's feet slip – on roads, for instance – or he stumbles on rough ground, sit still and don't try to pull his head up. He needs freedom to get back his balance.

Enjoy your hacking, and try to make it enjoyable for your pony, too. Thinking about how he is feeling on the ride will help you to understand his point of view – and ride him better.

Jumping

When you and your pony can manage several evenly-spaced trotting poles smoothly and confidently, your teacher can help you shorten your stirrups by one or two holes to give yourself a more springy position.

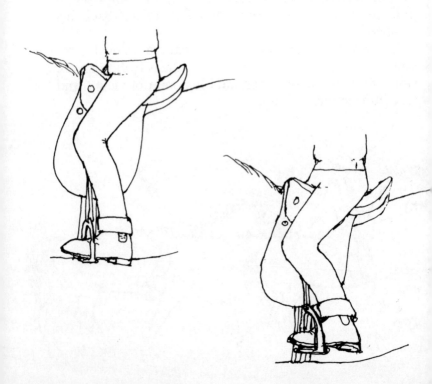

Keep your pony interested in the trotting poles exercise, by changing the number of poles and steps between. You will need a helper to alter the poles, because getting off each time to do it yourself would spoil the rhythm.

Don't have the poles too close or too far apart, or your pony will stumble over them. You should trot calmly towards them, over them and on again without hurrying or slowing down.

Now raise the last pole to about 10 inches (25 cms) off the ground. You will also need to move it a few inches further away from the other poles. Your pony will come trotting over the first few poles, then take a bigger step forward to get over the last one. You will feel an extra push from the pony's legs to lift him up and forward a little. This is the beginning of jumping. Remember the jumping position you've already practised over the trotting poles.

You could, of course, try this higher pole without the other trotting poles, but they are there to help you and your pony approach calmly, on an even stride. Practise several times, until you can do the exercise quite happily, then go round the other way. As you have changed direction, your helper will need to alter the poles, so that you come to the raised one last.

When you feel you are ready, and can manage to keep your pony straight and steady, remove the second pole from the end, and raise the last one a little more. Cavaletti, which are poles fixed on to crosses, are useful here, because they have only to be turned over.

Your pony will now begin at the trot, as before, but will probably change to a canter stride to hop over the last pole. Don't alter your position – just try to go with him, keeping your head up and your body level. Find something ahead of you to look at, so that you don't look down at the poles and spoil your balance.

If your pony canters for a few strides afterwards, keep your seat firmly in the saddle and push your heels down.

After you have tried it a couple of times, sit deep and ride your pony into a walk. Give him a pat and lengthen the reins to let him have a stretch. Never go on doing the same thing over and over again, because it is boring – especially for the pony.

Once it feels good and comfortable to hop over low poles, then you can try trotting over cavaletti on their own, placed here and there about the school. Also, crossed poles, supported on "drums" (empty containers, usually), are good jumps for beginners because they make you think about riding straight at the middle of them.

Three straw bales placed end to end make a nice jump (though greedy ponies might want to stop and have a chew!), and small logs are excellent, but do check that the landing and take-off places are safe if you're out on a hack.

Narrow jumps are not very easy – it's hard to keep absolutely straight at them – and flimsy ones are bad because ponies don't bother to pick their feet up properly, and stumble over them. So look for low, solid jumps that you know your pony will like.

Before you go on to higher jumps, practise over wider ones, such as low parallel poles (two poles, side by side).

As you become more experienced, you will want your pony to get used to more unusual obstacles. Try sacks or coats draped over the poles. They won't make the actual jump any bigger, but your pony will give a bigger jump because it looks funny.

Ponies also jump higher than they need to the first time they meet a wall – either a low part of a real wall, or the wooden, show-jumping kind. And they'll do the same with hedges and brush fences, however small. Surprisingly, they often give quite big jumps over ditches, too. Ponies are naturally afraid of holes in the ground, so when they come across a ditch – especially one with water in it – they'll sometimes dither on the edge, then jump much higher than is necessary.

Once they're used to all these different kinds of jump, they'll hop over them smoothly and easily, not wasting any energy. But it is sensible for a beginner to learn to jump on a pony which is already experienced.

However good and helpful your pony is, though, you are bound to get things wrong sometimes. You might come towards a jump too slowly, so that your pony isn't ready to lift himself over it, or too fast, so that he doesn't get a good look at it. Either way, he may stop unexpectedly in front of the jump. This is called "refusing".

Or he may "run out". This means swerving to one side, to miss the jump. It sometimes happens because he hasn't been ridden straight towards the jump, or is going too fast, or because his rider's reins are too long.

All this is a test of your riding position. If you keep your heels well down, and your seat down in the saddle, with your head up, you should stay in the right place. If you are out of position when the pony changes his movement suddenly, you may well end up sitting on the ground.

Wobbling off your pony will very likely happen from time to time, but it won't matter very much so long as you are wearing the right clothes to protect you. It will probably happen so quickly that you won't know until you're on the ground. Often, it's the surprise that makes people cry – not the hurt. And it all usually looks far worse than it actually is.

If you do fall off, take some deep breaths to help yourself get over the shock. Your helper will probably come and put an arm around you for a moment, because a bit of love always helps put people right. Then the two of you will have to catch your pony again. He may have been frightened by your fall, so talk calmly to him and reassure him. Even if his reins are dangling, don't run up to him – pick up a handful of grass to try to get him to come to you.

You may feel cross with your pony for causing the upset, but it's too late to tell him now – he won't understand. Sort yourself out and get back on top, then walk him quietly around for a bit. Think about what went wrong and talk with your teacher about it – *that* is the important part: to save it happening again.

Cantering

One day, when you have got on well with your ride and your pony has behaved well, ask your helper if you can sit on him bareback while he is led back to his field. Do this after the ride, not before, so that he is loosened up and relaxed. Feel the warmth and strength of his body beneath you as you sit tall and take hold of a handful of his mane. Your helper will be ready with a hand to steady you if you slip sideways. Being really close to the pony's movement is a lovely feeling – and it's that sort of closeness you should try to feel, even when there is a saddle between you and your pony.

You may, at your next lesson, be ready for the sitting canter. You will probably have felt the canter movement already, in a few strides after hopping over cavaletti. Perhaps, too, you will have tried a standing-up canter while hacking on a leading rein, and counted the change in rhythm from the "one-two, one-two" of the trot to the "one-two-three" of the canter.

Cantering is quite difficult to do well, so don't try it until you can easily manage a sitting and rising trot and simple exercises over trotting poles.

To find out what the canter movement is like, try it first on your own two feet, with one foot ahead of the other, in a circle. To keep your canter smooth and balanced, you'll find you need to lead with the leg nearest the middle of the circle. It's the same for your pony – he, too, should lead with the inside leg.

To help him do this, we must give him the right aids, or messages. It is best if you can practise this in a "school", which is a fenced-in riding area.

Ride him in a big circle at a steady trot, with your reins short. Push your seat as deep into the saddle as you can, without becoming tense. You can't go into a good, sitting canter from a stiff, uneven trotting movement. Keep your pony lively by tapping with both legs to send him forwards.

To begin with, try cantering just down the long side of your school. Come around the end in a smooth curve at a sitting trot, with your inside hand leading the inside rein a little away from your pony's neck, to help him bend gently into the curve.

Don't let the outside rein go slack, don't move your hands across the top of the pony's neck, and don't lean your body over.

Sit deep, with your inside leg on the girth and your outside leg slightly further back. Keep your heels down and your head up, and say "Can-ter!" firmly, as you send him on by tapping with both legs.

The canter doesn't have to be a faster pace than the trot – it's just a different rhythm, but if your pony is lazy you will have to send him strongly forwards to change to his canter stride. If you have a lively pony, give the aids especially gently and smoothly, so that he doesn't rush off. Keep your shoulders back, your head high and your hands still but not stiff. It may help at first to hold your neck-strap and to pretend there's a pound note under your bottom – try not to let it flutter away!

You will probably have to go on giving little taps with your legs to keep your pony going, but remember to keep your heels down all the time. If you are tense, your seat will come above the saddle, so relax and let yourself sink into the lovely, rocking-horse movement.

When you reach the end of the school, ride your pony into the trot again by sitting back and down and saying "Ter-rot!" or "Whoooa . . ." Squeeze with both legs and give a steady but gentle pull on the reins. It doesn't matter if he takes a few strides to "get the message". Try for smooth changes into the canter and back to the trot, not instant, jerky ones.

Later on, you can try cantering around a curve – perhaps right round the end of the school and up the other side. Because your pony is leading with his inside leg, he will tend to swing you slightly outwards on bends, so keep your inside leg especially well down. If you feel yourself tightening up, try to soften your muscles by moving your elbows or knees slightly. Remember the relaxed feeling of the pony's muscles when you rode him bareback – you want your body to feel the same.

Galloping is faster than cantering. The rhythm changes to a four-time beat: "da-dum, da-dum". You should use your jumping position, standing up in your stirrups. *However*, ponies usually find galloping rather exciting, and can be difficult to control, so don't ask your pony to gallop unless you are an experienced rider.

Exercises for Ponies and Riders

Whether you are learning to ride in a field or a specially-made "school", your pony will get very bored if you just ride round and round. It's important to change pace often – walk, trot, canter, halt – so that your pony has to pay attention, but you must remember to change direction sometimes, too.

Riding in a clockwise direction, you are riding on the *right rein*, because it is the right rein that is leading your pony around the corners. In an anti-clockwise direction, you are on the *left rein*.

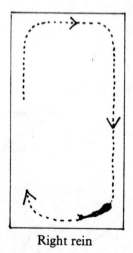

Right rein

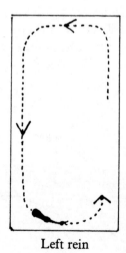

Left rein

Changing the rein means going round the other way, and you should do this quite often to stop your pony getting stiff and "one-sided" from always bending his body the same way.

One way to change the rein is to cross the school from corner to corner, through the middle, making a rounded "Z" shape. Your turns should be smooth curves. To help you remember where to turn, you can say to yourself: "Round the end, then round the bend" – you have to turn at the corner *after* the short side of the school, not before it.

Changing the rein

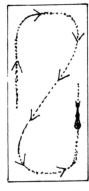

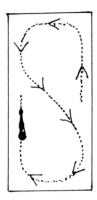

right to left   left to right

When you have changed the rein, ride around the edge of the school again. This is called *going large*.

Riding circles is very good for your pony. To move in a smooth, even circle, your pony's long shape has to be slightly bent all the time, following the line of the curve. This makes his inside hind leg work harder, by stepping further underneath him.

Keep both reins short enough to guide him with an even hold on both sides. "Feel" your inside rein and move it slightly away from his neck to begin the circle and to keep the curve of it. Send him forwards with both legs into this shape, but use your inside leg slightly more strongly, so that he bends around it a little. Your outside rein tells him how big you want the circle to be. Don't expect circles to be easy, because they're not. But practice helps a great deal.

Having completed your circle, straighten up and go large again, rejoining the track where you left it.

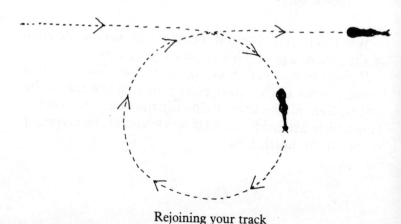

Rejoining your track

When you are riding well-shaped circles that are about the right size (covering half the school), you can try a *figure of eight*. Ride your circle towards the centre of the school, then change the rein by riding straight for two or three strides before calmly setting off to circle the other way, using the other half of the school. Try this movement at the walk first, then at a steady trot.

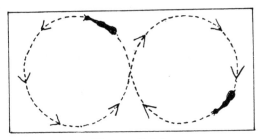

Figure of eight

Another exercise you can practise is *turning across* the school. The idea is to turn corners without the help of following the sides of the school. Ride along the side of the school, then turn away from the track and ride in a straight line across the middle. When you reach the other side, you can either stay on the same rein, or change it.

Riding these different shapes will help you to have more control over your pony. You will be practising the aids and exercising the pony's "bending" muscles – hard work for both of you, but interesting as well. There are many other exercises – some quite difficult – you may one day learn, but they are all built on these simple ones.

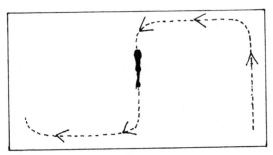

Turning across

Exercises for Riders

These are fun, too, and very good for you. You can do them at the standstill, with someone holding your pony. Knot your reins, so that they don't dangle, and drop your whip for the moment – don't throw it. Take your feet out of the stirrups.

All your joints (your ankles, knees, hips, shoulders, elbows, and those in your neck and back) are usually a bit stiff. Give them a wriggle . . . turn them . . . stretch them – then rest them. Just sitting up straight is a way of stretching – *stretching upwards*. If you also stretch one arm up in the air and your legs downwards, making them as long as you can, you'll feel as if you've grown inches.

Put your feet back into the stirrups and keep the lower half of your body in the correct riding position while you exercise your top half.

Begin with *toe-touching*. Hold the front of the saddle with one hand while you bring the other hand down to touch your toe. It doesn't matter if you can't quite reach – just bend down as far as you can. Don't bring your foot up to meet your hand. Now stretch your arm up high. Bend and stretch several times, to loosen up, then change to the other arm and foot. Try to keep your legs still.

Later on, do this exercise without holding the saddle, then try right hand to left foot, and left hand to right foot.

98

Another good exercise is this one, sometimes called *Aeroplanes*. Sit up straight, with your arms out at shoulder height, and turn the upper half of your body from side to side. Turn your head as well, but keep the lower part of your body still. Swing your arms slowly, so that you don't lose your balance, and try to turn a little bit further each time.

Stop before you get too tired, and have a good wriggle.

Now rest your hands on your thighs and try *leaning forwards* on the pony's neck, turning your face a little so that the peak of your cap is safely to one side. Keeping your legs as still as you can, come slowly up again and sit tall.

A more difficult exercise is *leaning backwards*, so that your head and shoulders come to rest on your pony's back. It's important not to stick your legs forward. Relax for a little while, then come up, keeping your knees bent and your heels down. This is very good for your tummy muscles, but you may at first need help getting upright again.

If you feel a bit funny, leaning back with nothing to see except the sky, move nearer to some trees. Being able to see something above you will help you keep your balance.

Now exercise the lower half of your body, keeping the upper part straight and still – sitting tall.

With your feet out of the stirrups, *circle your ankles* – it's surprisingly hard work.

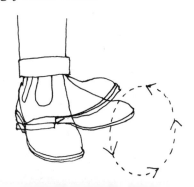

Now *swing your lower legs* backwards and forwards – this exercises your knees.

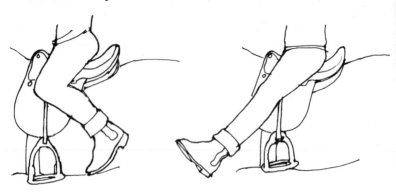

Your hip joints now – and this one's harder. *Lift your legs right off the saddle*, keeping them up for a few seconds (not too long – it's very tiring), then lower them. This exercise is especially good for you, because taking your legs off the saddle brings your seat as low as it can possibly be.

Here's one for fun. It's called *Round the World*. Lift a leg over the front of the saddle, and sit sideways. Now lift the other leg over the back of the saddle, so that you're facing backwards. Lift again to face the other side, and again to face the front again. Try to swing round smoothly, without kicking the pony, and keep your upper body upright.

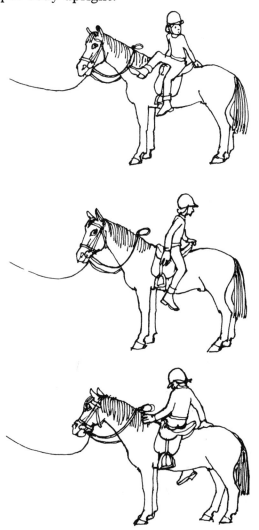

This exercise can be done first when you are standing still, then while you're being led at the walk. Put both reins into one hand, and take a handful of mane with the other hand. Now *stand up in your stirrups* and stay there, using your hold on the mane to help you balance. Stand as tall as you can, with your heels down and your feet back (otherwise you'll find yourself sitting down again). Keep your head up and stick your tummy out a bit, to stop yourself sagging in the middle. When you sit down, try not to move your legs from their balanced position.

Most ponies will stand quietly while you do your exercises, but you should never try them on a pony who isn't used to them – especially the leaning back exercise and Round the World.

You might like to know that children usually find these exercises much easier than adults, when they're learning – especially the hip exercise. Adults are inclined to moan and groan at that one!

Riding Lessons

Learning to ride should be a mixture of work and enjoyment. Trying too hard or endlessly practising may make you tired and tense, so that you can't ride well. On the other hand, all fun and games, with no proper teaching, won't make you a very good rider either. So lessons are best taken rather like your pony's food – little and often.

Everyone who wants to ride well needs help from an experienced person. Even beginners who are said to be "naturals" (which means that they balance well and move with the pony) need to be taught how to get their ponies to do what they want. If you haven't learnt how to control your pony – that is, getting him willingly doing what you want, and being firm if he tries to be naughty – neither of you will be safe and happy.

You may have lessons at a riding school, or with your own family at home, or with more experienced friends. You can also learn quite a lot by watching other people's lessons, studying good riders at horse shows and on television, and reading books about riding.

It's a big help if you can join your local Pony Club and take your pony to their rallies. These are a bit like pony parties – new friends to meet, new places to see and new people to help you. Most Pony Clubs will be happy to have you while you are still on a leading rein, and you'll be put into a group with other beginners. Lessons are usually split up by games and rests and chats about pony things.

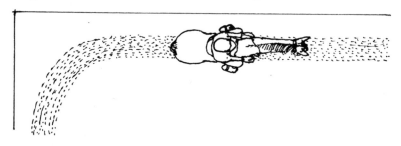

Sometimes a teacher will be very firm indeed, and this is nearly always for your own safety. If you are having difficulty controlling your pony, it can be hard to pay attention to your teacher. But you *must* try to listen and do exactly what you are told, however nervous you feel. Your teacher really does know how best to put things right.

One of the reasons why it's good to go to a riding school is that you'll find everything there that you need to help you learn.

To begin with, you'll ride in a proper "school": a closed-in area with a good ground surface – often wood shavings and sand. Slippery, muddy, uneven or stony ground is bad for ponies and can make riding much more difficult for you. As ponies don't concentrate very well if they're working in a big, open space, it's better if they're fenced in. This also helps you to feel safe and gives you straight lines to ride along.

A good school is at least 44 yards by 22 yards (40 metres long and 20 metres wide). It's helpful if it has letter markers around it, so that your teacher can tell you to "Halt at E" or "Trot at K", for instance.

If you are learning to ride in a field, always make sure that the gate is closed. You can place empty oil drums on the ground to show how big and what shape your riding area is to be.

When you are riding in a group, keep to the "outside track" and take special care so that you don't all get in a muddle. The "track" is where the pony's feet travel – keeping to the outside track means riding alongside the edge of the school and not wandering about.

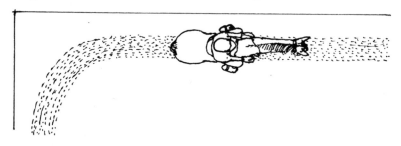

Your teacher will want to be able to see all of you in a group, not have some of you hidden behind each other or behind his or her back, so try to make your pony keep up with the others. If you find yourself lagging behind, turn across the school, or just cut across a corner to catch up. Don't upset your rhythm by speeding up or changing your pace.

If your pony walks more quickly than the one in front, mind he doesn't tread on the other pony's heels. You can imagine what damage that can cause. Also, most ponies don't like having others pushing up to their tails, and many will kick. (It helps if you pretend there's at least one invisible pony between you.) But don't spoil his nice, lively walk – either ride him into a circle, returning to the track where there's a space, or turn across the school to take over "leading file" (that's the person at the front of the group).

If you want to overtake, don't pass too close to the next pony or try to squeeze between him and the edge of the school. Turn clearly across the school on the inside of him.

When you are being taught in a group, try to obey all the instructions quickly and smoothly, so that later on you can ride more complicated movements together.

At the end of your lesson, make much of your pony: pat him, stroke him and talk to him. He'll be glad to see you next time.

Say "Thank you" to your teacher, whether he or she is a riding school instructor, or your mother or father, or a friend at home. Talk about how you felt during the lesson, what you liked or didn't like, and about what you would like to do in the future.

Having Fun with Your Pony

There are all sorts of different activities you can enjoy doing with ponies – and they can be fun for your pony, too.

Pony Trekking

When you can manage to go out hacking, with someone looking after you, you might like to plan a trek. This means riding a long way at a slow pace – usually over specially beautiful countryside. It's a lovely way to relax and look at scenery, and you can explore places you would never even see from a car. If you take headcollars you can stop for a rest – perhaps have a picnic, too. There are many trekking centres which offer holidays like this.

Riding Holidays

On some riding holidays you can have lessons in a school as well as going out hacking, and you'll also spend some time being taught how to look after the ponies.

The Pony Club

If you join the Pony Club you will find yourself invited to lots of exciting activities. As well as working rallies, there may be competitions, film shows, talks, treasure hunts, visits (to a racing stable, perhaps, or a blacksmith's) and Summer Camp, where you and your pony can go and stay for a week, having riding and pony care lessons and taking part in all kinds of fun.

Hunting and Hunter Trials

Hunting (sometimes called "riding to hounds") is a sport greatly enjoyed by those who can manage a pony at the gallop and who like riding across country. You do need to be well under control and have an experienced person with you who can keep an eye on you and explain the "rules" of hunting – like keeping quiet at the right times, staying off farmers' crops, and taking care not to ride too near the hounds.

Hunter trials are competitions where horses and ponies are ridden over a course of natural-looking fences at a steady gallop. Sometimes there are gates to be opened, or streams to splash through.

Shows and Gymkhanas

Hunting is a winter sport, and summer is the show season. You may already have been to a horse show – perhaps watched gymkhana events, too.

At a horse show, you will find that horses and ponies are entered for various different classes.

The *Showing* classes are really like ponies' beauty contests. They are judged partly on the animals' good looks, partly on their movement, which should be smooth and willing, and partly on their manners – and those of their riders!

If a class is judged on *turn-out*, the pony and rider have to be very smart and correct and spotlessly clean – lovely to watch, but very hard work to prepare for.

A *Family Pony* class is judged a bit like a showing class, but the ponies have to be suitable for all members of the family – strong enough to carry a grown-up, yet kind and gentle enough for a young child.

A *Working Hunter* pony has to be nice to look at and well-mannered, and should be able to gallop and jump well.

You've probably watched adult *Show-Jumping* on television. One of the reasons why the horses are brave enough to tackle the huge fences is that they have great confidence in their riders.

This trust between horse and rider can be found in all successful partnerships, but it can begin right from the start of your riding. Give your pony love, as well as firmness, and learn all you can, so that you both improve together, then your pony will be eager to do all that you want him to.

Your first efforts at show-jumping may be on a leading rein in a beginners' class. You will need a pony who has done it all before, and a leader who is energetic enough to leap over the jumps alongside you! Even if you don't win a prize, enjoy yourself, and don't forget a grateful pat on your pony's neck, and a "thank you" to him for helping to teach you.

Gymkhana events are races for ponies and their riders. They teach you to move about with your pony and ride naturally, while concentrating on something else, like not letting your egg wobble off its spoon in the Egg-and-Spoon race. And having to compete against others usually makes you try just that little bit harder.

Pony Rides

Pony-owners, or other people who are used to handling ponies, may be asked to help with pony rides at a village fête, and this is a wonderful way of letting plenty of children get the "feel" of ponies. For many children, it will be their first ride ever. Most of the "customers" won't be experienced riders, and will be wearing unsuitable clothes, so they'll need a lot of attention. Even if they think they can manage, they should be kept on a leading rein and not left to ride off on their own. The organiser should be too concerned with their safety and the ponies' comfort to take any chances.

An hour and a half of different children climbing on and off is usually quite enough for any pony's patience, so even if there's still a queue, put your pony's needs first and take him quietly home.

After the Ride

When you have finished riding – perhaps when you notice that your pony seems tired – take him back to his stable. Try to end his "work" on a good note – when he's done something well.

Never hurry back. The rule to remember is "Start slowly – work hard – finish quietly", whether you're having a lesson in the school or hacking out. He should be allowed to finish calm and cool, able to enjoy the rest that is his reward for working.

Ask your pony to halt properly, then dismount. Give him a good pat – maybe a titbit, too.

Now put your left arm through the reins so that you have both hands free to run the nearside stirrup up the underside of the stirrup leather and tuck the loop back through the stirrup. Let the girth down two holes, on both buckles, then go around the front and see to the offside stirrup.

Lift the reins over your pony's head and lead him round for a few minutes to relax. If he is hot and sweaty he will have to walk around for a bit longer.

Lead your pony into his stable, and put the reins back over his head. While you and your helper are unsaddling him, keep an arm through the reins so that he doesn't wander about. Stand on his near side and undo the girth straps completely, lowering the girth gently, so that it doesn't swing down and bang against his legs.

Now use both hands to lift the saddle towards you, on to your left arm, with the pommel nearest your elbow. With your right hand, catch the girth as it comes over the pony's back, and place it across the saddle (muddy side up, so that it doesn't scratch the leather).

Put the saddle down somewhere safe and pick up the headcollar.

To stop your pony walking away while you take off his bridle, your helper can hold the headcollar rope around his neck. Unfasten the noseband and the throat lash, so that everything behind the pony's face is undone. Now gather up the reins with the headpiece and lift them slowly up over his ears to remove the bridle. Wait for him to drop the bit from his mouth – never pull it, because this will hurt his jaw and teeth and frighten him.

When you have put on the headcollar, tie your pony up safely and return your saddle and bridle to their rack and peg for wiping over or thorough cleaning.

wisp

Give your pony a quick rub down with a wisp (a hard, thick plait of hay) or a big handful of loose straw. Rub sideways across the sweaty area where the saddle and girth were, and gently behind his ears, where the bridle went. Give him a quick slap with the wisp over the muscly parts of his body – this will make him feel very relaxed, with that lovely tingly feeling you get after rubbing yourself down with a bath towel.

If he is being turned out straight away, take him to his field, closing the gate before you take off his headcollar. He will probably have a good, satisfying roll, then go to his water trough.

If he is to stay in, he will need a full bucket of fresh water and a haynet. A pony whose skin is warm from normal exercise is in a perfect state for really thorough grooming, so, if he's not too tired, now is a good time to do it.

Afterwards, you and your helper can put on his rug, if he wears one, untie him and leave him to rest. If he has only had a quick brush down, go back in half an hour to check that he hasn't broken out in a cold sweat – tiny droplets of sweat appearing at the ends of the hairs. A cold sweat can easily lead to a chill, so rub him down thoroughly again and walk him round to dry him off.

If he has had a hard day – hunting, jumping or trekking, perhaps – you should return to him later, after he has had a rest, and check him over carefully for any bumps, scratches or swellings. Get help to deal with these properly, then remove the droppings from his bed, refill his water bucket and haynet and wish him a good night's sleep.

Understanding Your Pony

Your pony, rather like some two-footed friends, will not always behave in the way you expect. There may be all sorts of reasons for the particular mood he's in – a cheeky one, perhaps, or a cross one – and it will be up to you to try and be understanding. Sometimes you'll succeed, sometimes you won't.

But if *you* behave oddly, he will not understand at all. Try to treat your pony always in the same way, when you're riding him as well as when you're looking after him. For instance, don't let him stop on a ride and eat grass one day, then smack him for it the next.

Be thoughtful with your pony, and you can expect him
to be well-mannered, too. He should move over when
you ask him to, stand still to be mounted, and obey the
aids when you're riding him. Always make your wishes
clear to him first, then, if you still can't get him to listen,
ask someone more experienced to help you both.

If you're looking after ponies, handling them and
riding them, you must have somebody around who really
knows what they are doing – for the ponies' sake as well as
your own.

Always remember to thank your helpers, whoever they
are – a child who has opened a gate for you, or a grown-up
who has spent hours teaching you to ride. And don't
forget that a rider should *never* just get off at the end of a
ride and fling the reins to someone else. It's up to you
always to see that your pony's comfort and safety are
taken care of before your own.

There are all kinds of ways by which you can improve your riding and learn more about horses and ponies. Read books, and talk about them with an experienced person. Go to different teachers for lessons – each one will add something new to your knowledge. Go and chat to your local feed merchant, blacksmith and saddler, and see what you can learn from them.

If you can, arrange to visit a stud, where you will see mares and stallions, and find out something about the behaviour and care of foals.

At race meetings, you'll see thoroughbred horses doing what they were first bred for – galloping like the wind.

Watch dressage demonstrations, when carefully trained, balanced horses show off their beautiful movements, often in time to music, rather as if they were dancing.

Superbly fit horses and riders can be seen taking part in Horse Trials – like the famous ones at Badminton – where they compete in three different activities: Dressage, Cross-Country and Show-Jumping.

Go to horse shows and gymkhanas and look at all the different breeds of pony. See how many you can recognise. Watch a side-saddle class and notice how it is still balance and moving with the horse that matters – the same as when riding astride.

Look at driving turn-outs, with their lovely bright, clinking harness and smart carriages. Maybe one day you will try this different way of moving together with your pony.

You're on the way to becoming a horseman – someone who understands horses and ponies and how to care for them, someone who can ride. Think of your first riding lessons as the early stages of dressage, your first time hacking out as the beginning of cross-country riding. Aim high. To be a good rider, you'll need plenty of effort, time, money and help, but it'll be worth it. Remember, though, that even a good rider can be a better one. There is always something new to be learnt.

Index